Microsoft®, Word®, Excel®, Outlook®, and PowerPoint® are registered trademarks of Microsoft Corporation.

Conventions used:

Keys to be pressed are enclosed in parenthesis such as: press (Enter).

Text to be typed, when included in an exercise step will be shaded, for example:
Type *No Fault Travel* and then press (Enter).

Be sure to check out our website: www.LutherMaddy.com to contact the author and see other resources available for this workbook.

Table of Contents

Lesson #1: Basic Text Formatting

In this lesson you will learn to:

Use Paragraph and Page Borders
Shade paragraphs
Use Styles
Use Newspaper columns
Create a Newsletter

Lesson #1: Basic Text Formatting

Formatting Text

In this first lesson you will begin creating a newsletter. You will continue to enhance it throughout the next few lessons. In this lesson you will learn to add shading, borders and other formatting options to text. The new features you are learning work just like the other font options you've learned. To enhance new text turn on the option and type. To change existing text, select the text and then apply the enhancement. In this portion of the lesson you will begin the creation of a simple newsletter.

Before we begin the newsletter we need to do a little housekeeping. We're going change some paragraph settings to ensure that we control the line spacing rather than MS Word. You'll do this through the Paragraph dialog box.

1.   **First, click the View Tab and turn on the Ruler if it is not displayed.**
We'll use the ruler to set tabs in this lesson.

2.   **Click the Paragraph dialog box launcher on the Home tab to display the Paragraph dialog box.**

3.   **Ensure that the Before and After spacing are both set to 0 pt and ensure the Line spacing is set at Single and click OK.**

By default, MS Word adds 10 points after each paragraph and a few extra points after each line. With this document we want to be completely in control of the spacing. As you use Heading Styles throughout this workbook, you may have to repeat the process below as Word may change the paragraph spacing back to the default setting when you apply a Heading Style.

4.   Now, display the Page Layout tab and click the Margins tool in the Page Setup group. Select Narrow from the Margins choices.

This will change the top, left and right and bottom margins to .5".

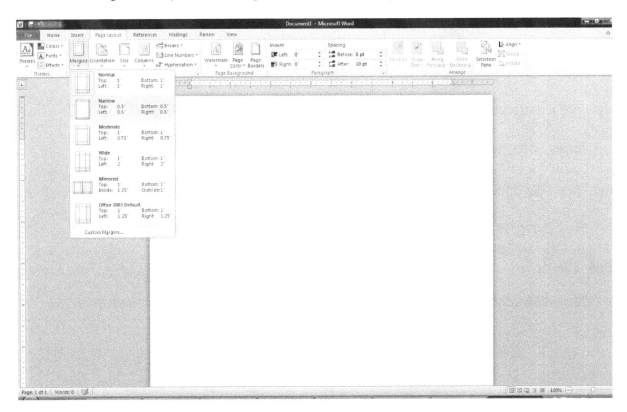

We'll want to use as much of the page as possible for our newsletter which is why we have decreased the margin size.

5.   Move back on the Home tab and change the font face to Arial and the size to 18 points. Then, center and type *Travel Tales* and press (Enter).

In case you forgot, you can find the Center align tool in the Paragraph group on the Home tab.

6.	On the next line, change the font size to 11 points. Then, turn on the Italics, type *A No Fault Travel Publication* and then press (Enter).

The above illustration shows the document using the Page Width view.

## 7.	Now, change the alignment to Left and turn off Italics.

Remember that once you turn on an enhancement it stays on until you turn it off.

## 8.	Set a right tab as close to the right margin as possible.
Don't set this tab beyond the margin. This tab will give you the ability to "flush right" text on this line.

To set a right tab, click the tab type tool to the left of the ruler until is displays a right tab. Then, click on the ruler where you want the tab set.

## 9.	Type *Volume 1* and then press (Tab).
You will have now moved to the right tab you set earlier. The text you type here will be right aligned.

## 7.	At the tab stop, type *January 1, 2014* and press (Enter).

Quickly Drawing Lines

You'll now draw a line below the text you just typed. To do this, you could choose Line from the Shapes tool on the Insert tab. However, this time you'll use a shortcut to quickly create a line.

8. Make sure the Insertion point is below the last line of text. Then type three dashes (---) and press (Enter).

You should now see a line directly below the text.

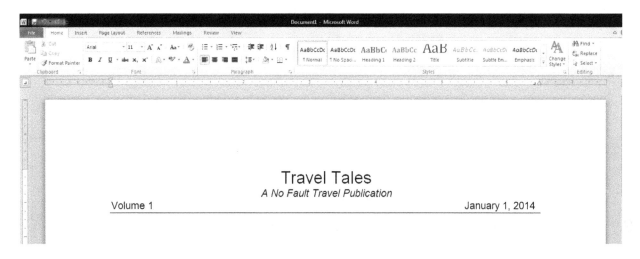

9. Press (Enter) to create an additional text line below the line you just drew.

Working with Section Breaks

After creating the newsletter's heading, you will want the text of the newsletter in columns. To create a page that has some text in columns and some not in columns, we'll have to use section breaks. Section Breaks allow us to drastically change formatting from one place to another, whether it is on the same page or on another page. You will now create a Section Break so you can place the text below the heading in two columns.

1. Click the Breaks tool on the Page Layout tab.

You should now see several different types of breaks that you can insert into this place in the document. At first glance, since we are going to place text in columns, the Column break seems like a good choice. However, this break creates a new column after the first column has been "filled up".

Some of the break types allow you to change formatting between pages. We want to change the formatting on the same page and the Continuous break lets us do that.

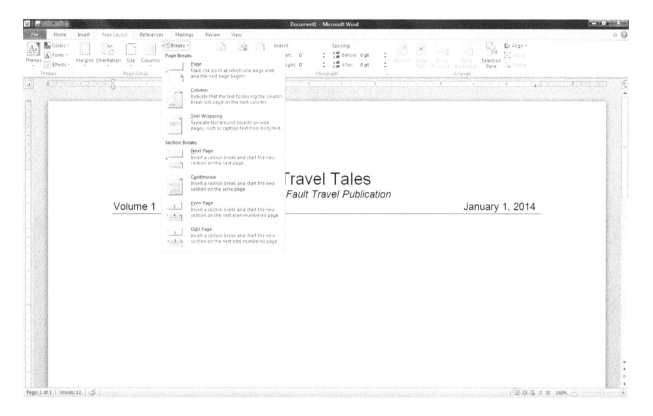

2. In the list of Breaks, choose Continuous.

You have now created a Continuous Section Break at this position in the document. At first glance, you will probably not notice any difference on the page. If you have previously modified your Status Bar display, you would then see Section 2 on the status bar. We're going to show you another way to see the section without having to change the Status Bar display. We'll do that by temporarily switching into Draft view.

3. Display the View tab and select Draft in the document views group.

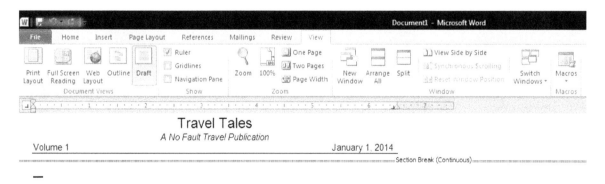

The Draft View allows you to see that Word has inserted a Continuous Section Break at this place in the document. If this section break were not here and you told Word to create two columns in this document, as we are about to do, the entire document would be placed in columns, including the newsletter heading. By placing a Section Break here, the columns will begin after the Section Break. The Section Break, in a sense, blocks the formatting changes from parts of the document we do not want changed.

Using Columns

After creating a Section Break where you want to begin using columns, the next step is to turn on the column mode. In doing so, you will also inform Word of how many columns you wish to use. In this case, you will use only two columns for the newsletter.

1.   Change the View back to Print Layout. Then, locate and click the Columns tool on the Page Layout tab.

As soon as you click this tool, Word will display a list of column numbers.

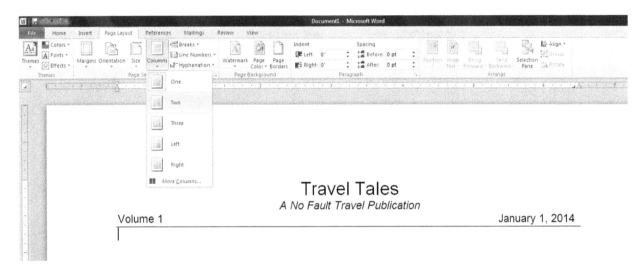

2.   Choose Two columns from the list of column choices.

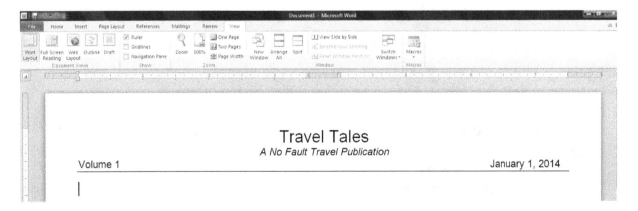

If you examine the ruler, you will note that it shows that you are using two columns. Because you inserted the Continuous Section Break, the newsletter heading stayed in single column mode. From this point on, the text you type will be in two columns.

Using Styles

Styles give you the ability to ensure that text has a consistent look throughout your documents. For example, assume this newsletter spanned several pages and included numerous articles. Assume you wanted the article headings to stand out from the rest of the text and did this by changing the font size. It is possible that over several pages and perhaps several days of creating the document you may forget if you were using 14 point or 15 point size for the article headings. By using a style, all the article headings will be consistent. And, if you later change your mind and decide the headings should be a different color, if you've used styles, all you have to do is redefine the style and all the headings will change instantly. In addition to consistency, using styles increases your productivity by making formatting changes quicker and easier.

For this newsletter example, you will use styles for the article headings.

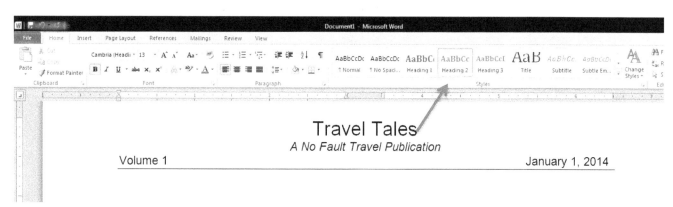

1.   Choose Heading 2 from the Styles section in the Home tab.

If the Navigation Pane displays, turn it off in the View tab.

2.   After choosing the Heading 2 style type: *Australia is a bargain!* and press (Enter).

The Heading 2 Style turned off automatically when you pressed (Enter). You can verify this by noticing that the Normal style is selected in the Styles group.

3.   Now, type the following paragraphs, press (Tab) before each paragraph:

> *If you've ever considered traveling to Australia, this is the time. Fares have never been lower and a strong US dollar means your in-country costs will be very low too.*
> *Don't miss this once in a lifetime chance to see the wildlife and scenery of this amazing continent.*
> *Call us for more details.*

As you type these paragraphs you should notice that the lines break at the end of the column rather than at the end of the page.

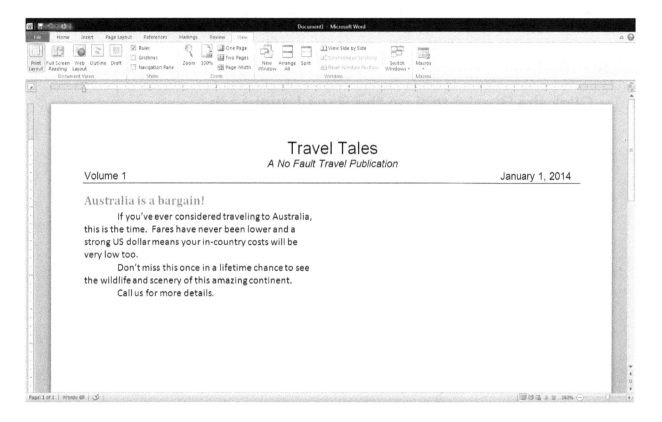

4. **One line below the text, press (Enter) then choose the Heading 2 style again.**

You're now going to create a second article.

5. **On the next line type: *Extreme Travel! – The Family Vacation* and press (Enter).**

6. **Now type the following paragraphs, pressing (Tab) before each:**

If you crave adrenaline rushes, try a cross-country driving vacation. We're not talking about a 2-hour drive. No, this needs to be at least 2 weeks long. The car needs to be as small as possible. And, you can't forget the children: at least two. Make sure the children can't stand each other and, by all means, make sure they don't want to go on this vacation either. Throw in a mom and dad who can't agree on anything and you've got the perfect Extreme travel situation.

If you survive this year's extreme vacation, come see us before next year and we'll show you how to save your sanity by flying to your ultimate destination.

7. **Press (Enter) after the last paragraph.**

Inserting Columns Breaks

You are now ready to begin the next column. If you had filled up the first column entirely, Word would automatically create a second column. However, since you have not filled the entire column, you must manually create a new column. You will do this by inserting a Column Break.

1. Click the Breaks tool on the Page Layout tab.

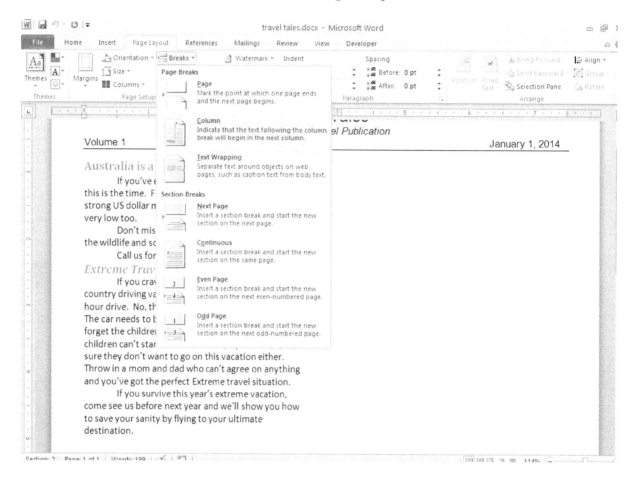

2. In the list of Breaks, choose Column break.

The insertion point should now be at the top of the second column. Don't worry about the insertion point being higher than where the text in the first column starts. The Heading 2 style you used for the article heading inserts extra space before the text. When you add an article heading here, it will match the other, providing you use the same style.

3. Display the Home tab and choose the Heading 2 style and type: *Looking for adventure? Take the bus!* and then press (Enter).

Once again, Word changes the style back to Normal when you press (Enter). You should also notice that the headings in both columns 1 and 2 start at the same position on the page.

4. **Now, type the following paragraphs:**

Once mainstay transportation providers, busses have fallen considerably in popularity. To revitalize the industry, bus companies are offering drastic discounts.

Traveling by bus allows you the opportunity to see neighborhoods that you usually miss when visiting certain cities. And consider the adventure of sitting for hours, or even days, beside someone who you would try desperately to avoid under different circumstances.

See the America that really is. Ride the bus.

Modifying Styles

If document text uses styles, you can then modify the style and all the text using that style will change to reflect the changes you made to the style. This is one significant advantage to using styles. In this portion of the exercise you will change the appearance of all the article headings in this document by modifying the style.

1. **In the Styles group of the Home tab, right+click Heading 2, then choose Modify from the shortcut menu.**

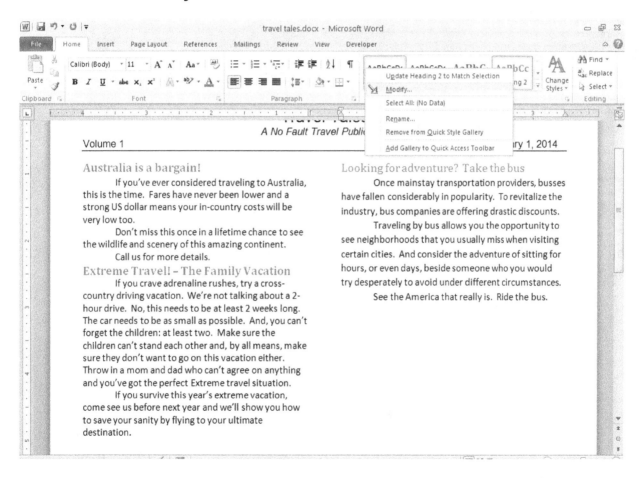

You will see the Modify Style dialog box. Here you can change the appearance of a style.

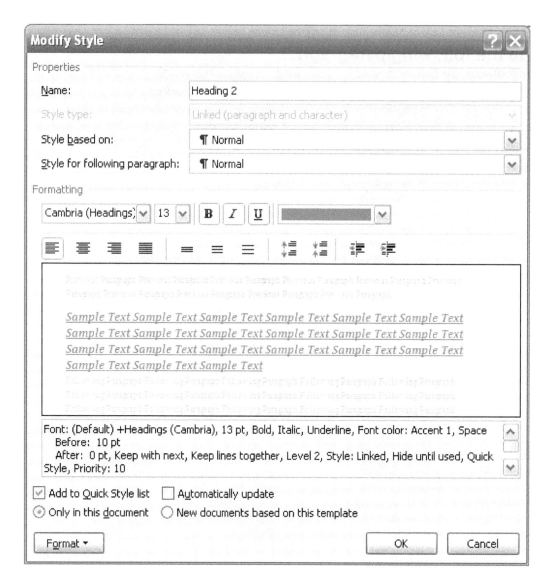

2. In the Modify Style dialog box, add Italics and Underlining, then click OK.

You should see that all the text using the Heading 2 is now formatted with the changes you just made.

Using Borders and Shading

You can easily draw attention to portions of your text by adding shading, borders or both. In this portion of the exercise you will add both page and paragraph borders. You can access shading and borders from the Format menu. To add borders or shading to more than one paragraph at a time you must first select the text you wish to enhance.

1. Select the heading and text relating to *Extreme Travel.*

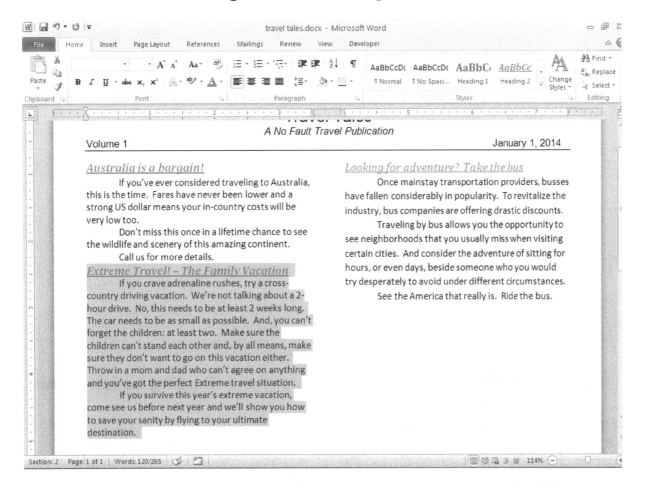

2. In the Home tab, click the arrow to the right of the Borders tool to display the Borders drop down list.

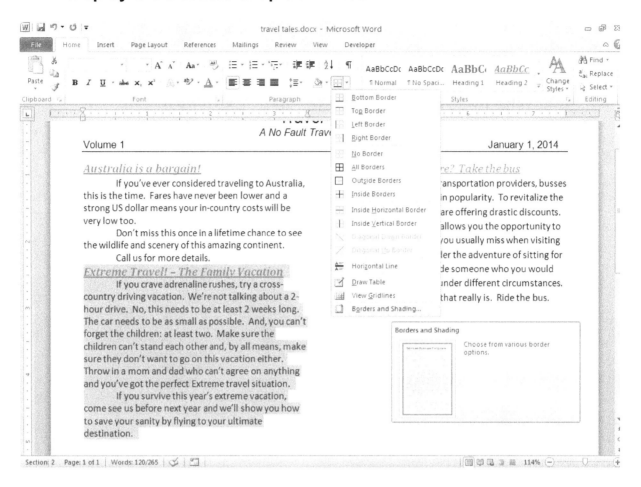

3. In the list of borders, click the Borders and Shading option at the bottom of the list.

You should now see the Borders and Shading dialog which that will allow you to select more options than using the tools on the Ribbon. You could have easily selected a border by choosing one of the options in the list, however, choosing this option allows you to select many additional options to Borders and Shading.

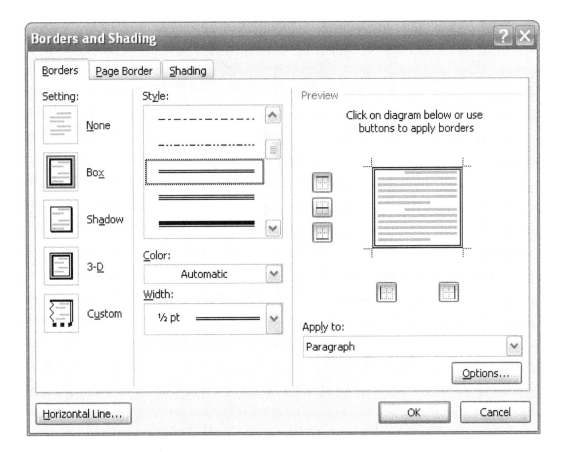

4. **Click the Borders tab if necessary, then choose Box as the border style. Scroll down the list of line Styles and select the double line.**

There are several border options you can select from here. Make sure the Apply to options has Paragraph selected since you do not want this border option on the entire page.

Stay in this dialog box because, as its name implies, you can also use it to choose shading options. You will now add some shading to the article you selected in this newsletter.

4. Click the Shading tab.

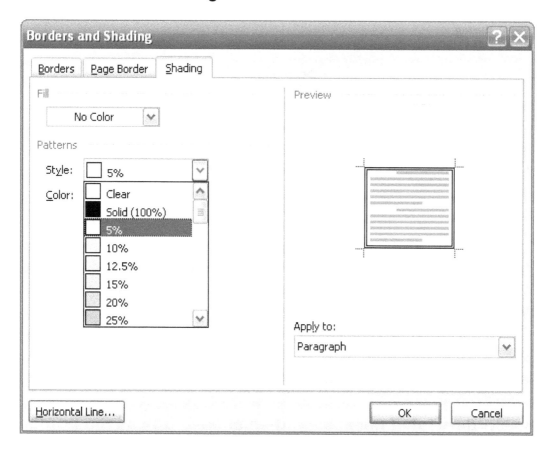

5. Choose 5% gray as the fill and click OK.
When you click outside the selected text you should see it has been formatted with the border and shading options you specified.

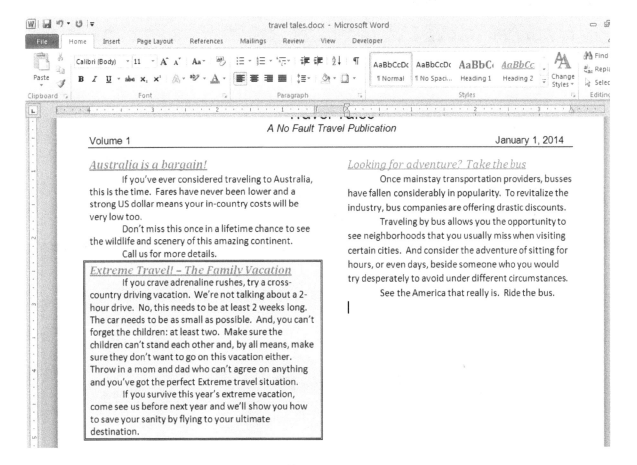

6. Save the file as _Travel Tales Newsletter_.

Creating a New Style

In this point in your document you've used some of the pre-existing styles in Word. While there are many pre-defined styles to choose from, there may be times you want to create your own style. In this portion of the lesson you will create your own style to use whenever you need text formatted in a consistent manner. As an example the exercise steps in this book use a custom created style.

To create a new style, you'll start with the newsletter heading and create a style from it.

1. **Select the newsletter heading, _Travel Tales_. Change its font color to Red and Italicize it. Leave the text selected.**

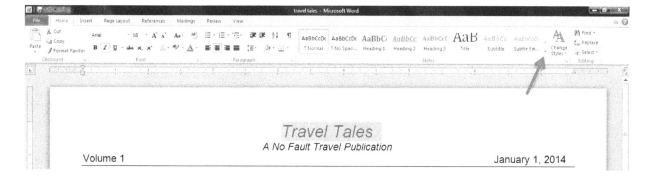

2. **Click the More arrow in the Styles group to display the Styles dialog box.**

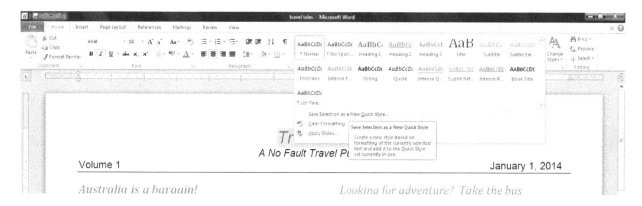

3. **Click the *Save Selection as a New Quick Style* option.**

You'll now see the Create New Style from Formatting dialog box. Here you'll name the style and choose additional options for the style.

4. **Name the style *Newsletter Heading* and then click the Modify button.**

Word now displays the Create New Style from Formatting dialog box. Here you can manually change some of the formatting options for this style such as size, color and so on. Some of the other important options you can select here are the Style Type, Style

Based on and the Style for the following paragraph. You can also specify whether this style should be available in all new documents (template) or just this one document.

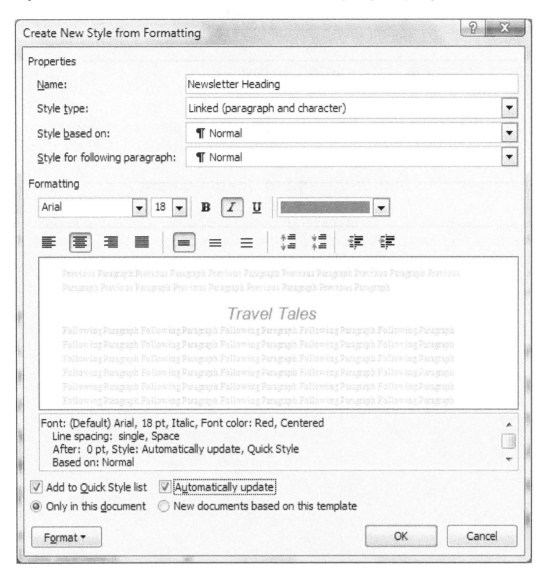

5. Change the *Style for the following* paragraph to Normal.

If you do not change this option to Normal, the style will continue until you turn it off. You may recall that as you created this newsletter, the Heading styles automatically turned off when you pressed enter. By choosing Normal for the following paragraph, that is what you are telling Word you would like to do when using this style as well. If this were a style you were going to use for many paragraphs of text rather than a one line heading, then leaving the style on, even after pressing Enter would be desirable.

6.   Click the Automatically update check box.

You have now told Word that you want all text in your document using this style to change automatically if you change the appearance of any of the text that uses this style.

7.   Click OK to complete the creation of this style.

You'll now add some additional text to your document to see how this new style works.

8.   Move the insertion point to the end of the document.

Remember, you can use (Control+End) to quickly move to the bottom of the document. When you do move the insertion point to the end of the document you should notice that it remains in the second column. You would like the text you are about to type to appear below the columned text so you will need to create a new section with only one column below that text.

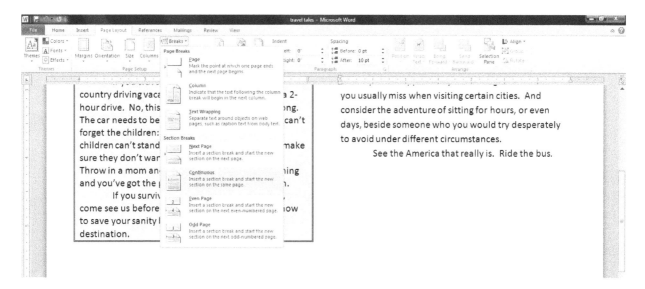

9.   Click the Breaks tool on the Page Layout tab and choose Continuous Section Break.

You should notice that the insertion point is below all the columned text. Looking at the Ruler (View, Ruler if it is not displayed), you should see that this position in the document still has two columns. Now you'll need to change the layout back to only one column.

10. Click the Columns tool and select 1 column. Next, choose Newsletter Heading from the Styles box and type: *No Fault Travel*

Automatically Updating Styles

Since you selected the Automatically Update option when you change the formatting options of text that uses this style, all text using that style will change.

The text you just typed should have the same formatting options as the text you used to create the Newsletter Heading style.

11. **Select the text you just typed at the bottom of the page and change the text color to Blue. After making this change, move to the top of the document.**

Both this line and the line you used to create the style will change automatically because you chose the Automatically Update option when you created the style. You have now permanently changed the style. Every time you use this style the text will be Blue.

12. **Erase the line you just typed at the bottom of the page, change the Style back to Normal, then save and close the Newsletter document.**

1.   Create the newsletter shown below.

Joe's Computer School

Classes for the Masses

Volume 8   June 1, 1999

Intro to Computers will get you going

Don't know a mouse from a rat? If not, sign up for our Intro to Computers class. We'll have you counting bits and bytes in no time.

Call for details.

New versions released daily!

It seems just when you get a software package learned, the company releases a new and entirely different version. If you find yourself struggling to learn a new version of a program you used to know, give us a call. We'll get you back to the comfortable stage.

Voice input making progress

More and more companies are releasing voice input devices and software. Their ultimate goal is to someday replace the keyboard. While the current devices are good if you have no keyboard skills at all, they still have a way to go to replace the keyboard entirely. In the meantime, keep practicing your typing.

2.   Save it as *Joe's Newsletter* and then close it.

Check Yourself

Questions:

1. What do Right aligned tabs do?
2. How do you create newspaper columns?
3. What is the purpose of Section Breaks?
4. How do you modify a style?
5. What are some advantages to using styles?

Lesson #2: Working with Images

In this lesson you will learn to:

Use Clipart images
Format images
Modify images

Lesson #2: Working with Images

Inserting Images

You can insert images two ways, from a file or from Clipart. Word's Clipart Gallery provides an easy way to view the images before you insert them. Word also gives you the ability to add useful images to your clipart gallery. In this lesson you will use the clipart gallery and insert an image from a file.

1.   Open the Travel Tales Newsletter.

2.   Display the Insert tab and click the Clip Art.

Finding Clipart Images

As you can see from the Clipart Gallery, there can be many images to select from. When you are looking for a particular type of image you can use the find command. The Search command will look for keywords in the name or description of the image. In this portion of the lesson you will use the search command to find an appropriate image for the Australia section.

1.   Click in the first line under the heading, Australia is a bargain.

Make sure your cursor is again the left margin. You can move it there by pressing the Home key if needed. Word will insert images at the position of the insertion point. This is why you moved the insertion point under this heading and to the left margin.

2.   Click in the Search for clips text box, type *kangaroo* and then press (Enter).

Word will now search the clipart gallery and locate the images that may in some way relate to "kangaroo".

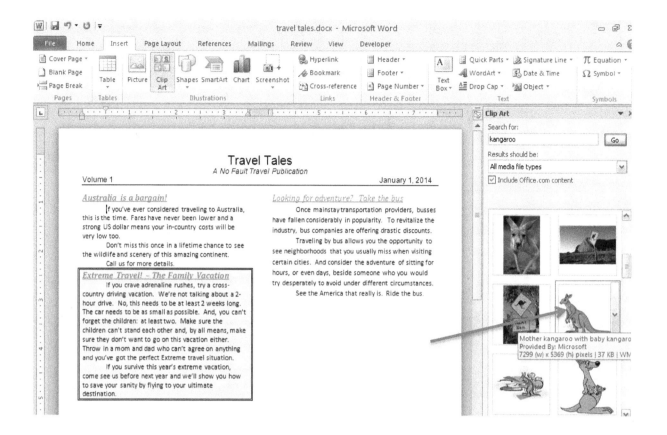

3. Click on an image similar to the one in the second column above to insert the clip into the document.

Clipart galleries vary widely from one computer to another. If you don't have kangaroo images, just choose any image you like.

4. Close the Clip Art task pane after inserting the image.

You closed the clip art task pane simply to give you move working room with your document. There is no harm in leaving it open.

Adjusting Image Attributes

The image is now inserted in its normal size. In this case, the normal size is too large for this document. You will now adjust the size and other attributes of this image. To do this, you can right+click on the image. Then from the image shortcut menu, choose Size and Position.

1. Right+click the kangaroo image you just inserted.

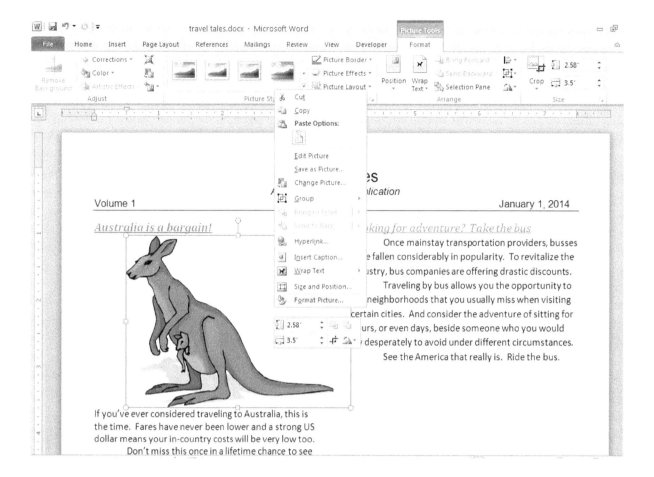

2.   Choose Size and Position from the image shortcut menu.

You will now see the Layout dialog box. Here you can make changes to the image, including its size.

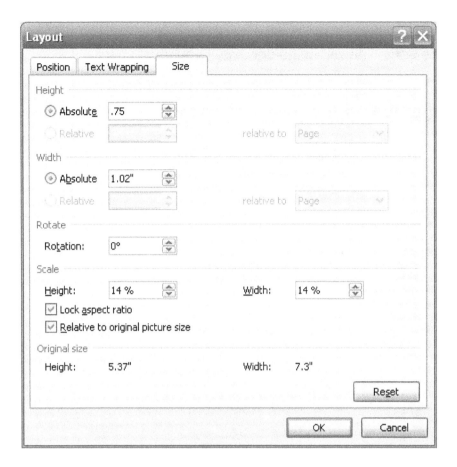

3.   **Make sure the lock aspect ratio check box is on. Then, change the Height setting to .75". When you click in the Width section, you should notice that Word changed it automatically for you. Click OK when done.**

The Lock aspect ratio will cause the width to change with the height to keep the original image's proportions.

You should notice that the kangaroo image is smaller. You should also notice that the text does not wrap beside it. The way the text wrapping is set by default, the image is treated like a letter of text. The text stays in line with the image instead of wrapping beside it. You will now change the wrapping style to allow the text to wrap beside the image. You will have Word change the position of this image so it is in line with the starting point (left) of the column.

Image Wrapping

As the image is now, simply making it smaller will not allow text to move beside it. To get the image and text in the same line within the document you must change the wrapping style.

1.   **Right click the kangaroo image and select Size and Position again.**

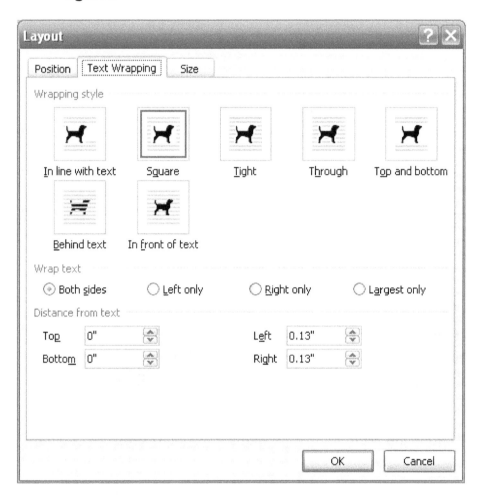

2.   **Click the Text Wrapping tab and choose Square wrapping then click the Position Tab.**

3. **In the Position tab, click the Alignment radio button in the Horizontal section and choose Left relative to Column. And click OK.**

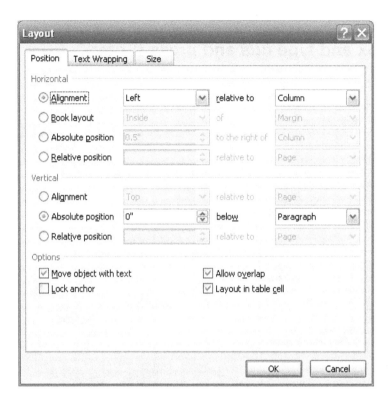

You should now see the image and the text in the same line. The text wrapped beside the image. The image should also be against the left margin if it was not before. It may be necessary to move the image back down into the paragraph.

With some images you may wish to choose Tight. This would cause the text to contour around the image within the image's box.

3. **Move the insertion point to the beginning of the line of text just below the article heading for *Looking for Adventure?***

You will now insert another image in this article.

4. **Click the Clip Art tool on the Insert tab.**

5. **Click in the Search textbox and type *bus* and press (Enter).**

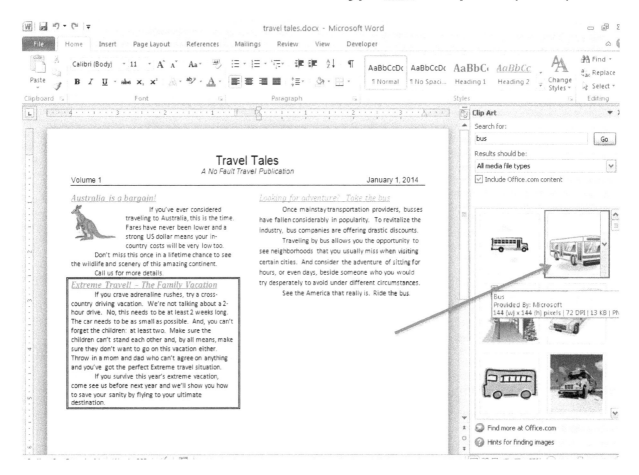

6. **Click the bus (or similar to) the one shown above to insert the image into the document.**

You will now change the size and position of this image but using the ribbon instead of the shortcut menu.

7.   Click the Format tab from the Picture Tools ribbon.

8.   In the Size group, change the Width of this image to 1.25".

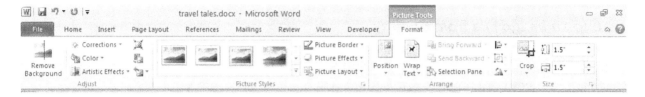

Don't change the height. As long as the Lock Aspect Ratio option (default setting) is on the height will change automatically to 1.25, if you have used this image.

9.   With the bus picture still selected, click the Wrap Text drop down list and choose Square as the Text Wrapping style in the Arrange group.

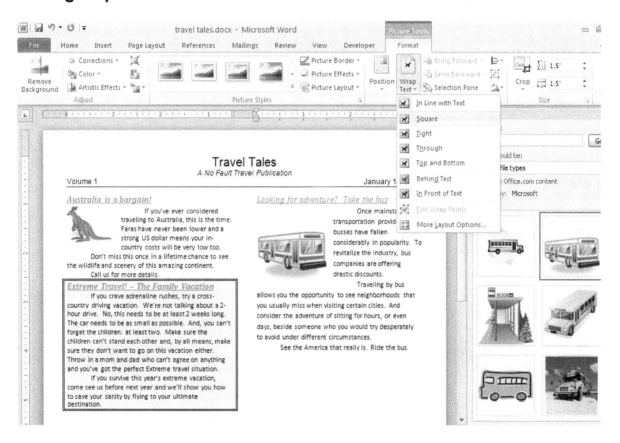

10.   Click the Position drop down list and choose More Layout Options. Change the horizontal alignment to Left of Column as you did for the kangaroo.

You changed this setting to ensure that the bus image will begin at the left edge of the second column in this newsletter

Inserting an Image from File

If you have scanned an image, downloaded one from the internet, or created it in a program such as Paint, this image will be a file rather than in the clipart gallery. In this portion of the exercise you will insert an image from file.

Creating an Image File from Clipart

To ensure that you have the same or similar image to what this text will use in the next few steps, we'll have you create an image file from a Clipart image. Then, you can insert this image into your document. As you are using Word to create your own documents, you'll have your own image files to use.

1.   Create a new, blank document with Control+N.

You'll use this blank document to insert a clip art image and then save it as a picture file. After you've done that, you'll insert it into your Travel Tales document.

2.   Display the Insert tab and click the Clipart tool.

3.   Type *Tropical* in the Search for box then locate and insert a picture similar to the one below.

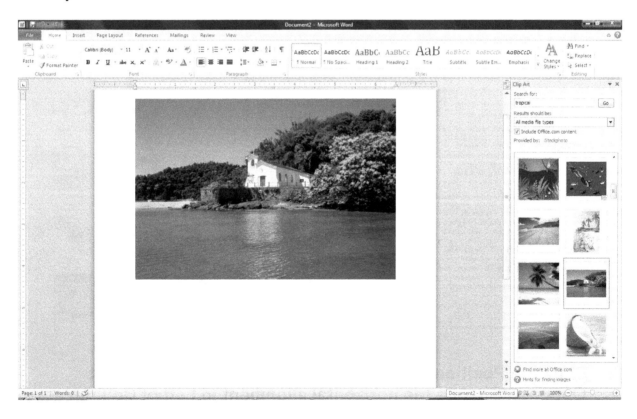

It will not matter if you do not have the exact picture we've used here.

4. Right+Click the image you just inserted and choose Save As Picture from the shortcut menu.

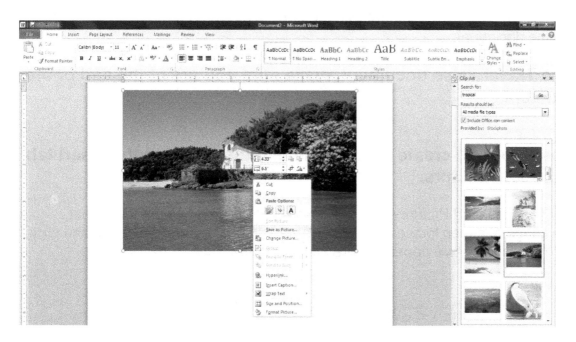

You should now see the File Save dialog box, which may appear differently depending on your version of Windows.

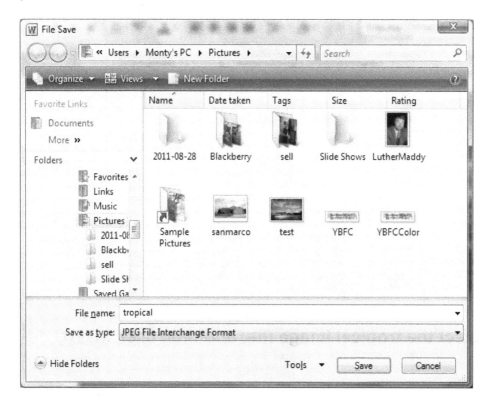

5. Enter *tropical* in the file name textbox and click Save.

You have now saved this clip art image as a picture file to use with the rest of this lesson.

6. **Close the document with the picture without saving and return to the Travel Tales document.**

You did not need to save the document with the tropical picture because you saved the picture from the document.

7. **In the Travel Tales document, make sure you are at the end of the document .**

8. **Press (Enter) to create a blank line and then display the Insert tab and choose Picture.**

You will now see the Insert Picture dialog box. Here you will first find the folder that contains the image and then locate the image. After finding the image, select it and click Insert. Your images folder will appear differently than this.

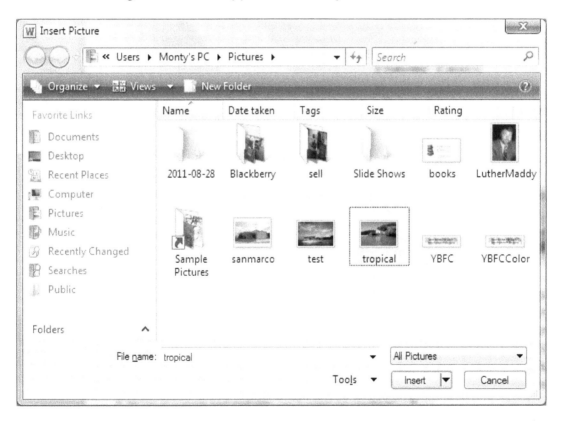

5. **Locate and select the tropical image file, and then click Insert.**

You should now see the image on a second page of the newsletter. This is because the image is currently too large to fit on the first page. You will now resize the image so it fits on the first page of the newsletter.

Positioning and Sizing an Image by Dragging

Up to this point you have sized and positioned images using the Format tab on the Picture Tools ribbon. This method is best when accuracy is important. For less accurate adjustments, you can move and or size by dragging the image. To move an image by dragging, the wrapping style cannot be in line with text. And, since this is the default mode, you will need to change the wrapping style.

To move an image, move the mouse pointer into the image's center and just click and drag. To size an image, locate a sizing handle on an edge and then click and drag.

Resize: ⟷   Move: ⬌⬍

1.   **Make sure the image is selected. (You'll see sizing handles around the image.)**

2.   **Move to the bottom right corner of the image and then click and drag up and left to reduce the size of the image to approximately 2" tall.**
You can use the vertical ruler to help you with sizing this image.

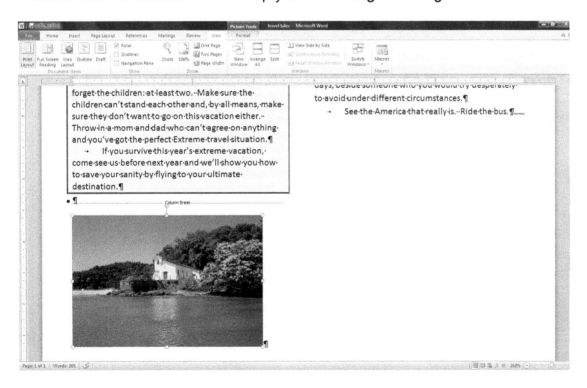

3. Use the Wrap text tool on the Format tab to change the Wrapping style to Square.

4. Use the four-headed arrow to move the image to the right of the page as shown below.

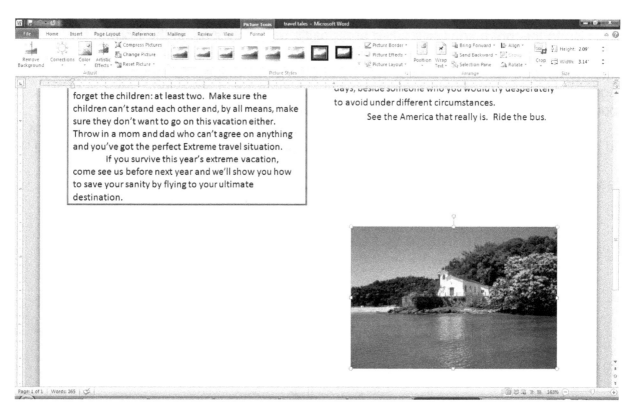

Dragging an image does not easily allow accurate placement. If you want the image placed exactly, you should use the Size and Position Layout dialog box.

4. Save and close the newsletter.

1.   Open Joe's Newsletter.

2.   Insert and format the Clipart images as shown.
Use these or similar images. You may have to experiment with the size to get the images to fit properly.

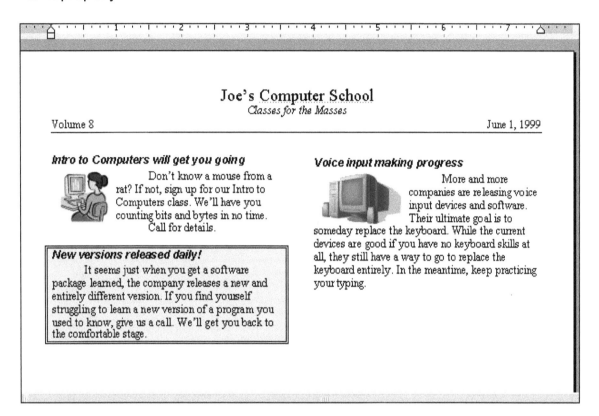

3.   Save and close when done.

Lesson #3: Working with Shapes

In this lesson you will learn to:

Create and edit AutoShapes
Group shapes
Modify shapes
Turn a shape into an image file

Lesson #3: Working with Shapes

Word allows users to create a large variety of shapes. After creating these shapes you can then modify and add options to the shapes to change their appearance even more. In this lesson you will create a new Logo for the No Fault Travel agency.

1.   Create a new blank document.

Remember you can use (Control+N) or use the File menu to create a new document. It will not matter if you have any other documents open at the moment.

Using WordArt

The WordArt feature allows you to easily and quickly create impressively formatted text. There are several WordArt styles to choose from and even these can be modified. You find WordArt after opening the Insert ribbon and choosing WordArt from the Text group.

2.   Click the WordArt tool on the Insert Tab.

You should now see a list of the WordArt styles you can choose from.

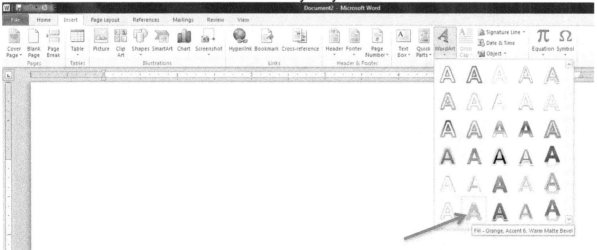

3. In the WordArt gallery, choose the second style from the left in the last row.

You should now see that Word has inserted a text box into your document. Here you simply type the text you want displayed as WordArt.

4. In the WordArt textbox box, type *No Fault Travel* and then click outside the textbox.

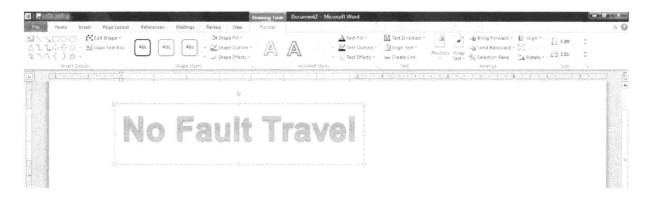

Combining Shapes

Our ultimate goal is to create a graphic logo for our company, No Fault Travel. We have created the graphic text, but now we'll add another shape, a rounded rectangle to the WordArt text to make it appear more impressive.

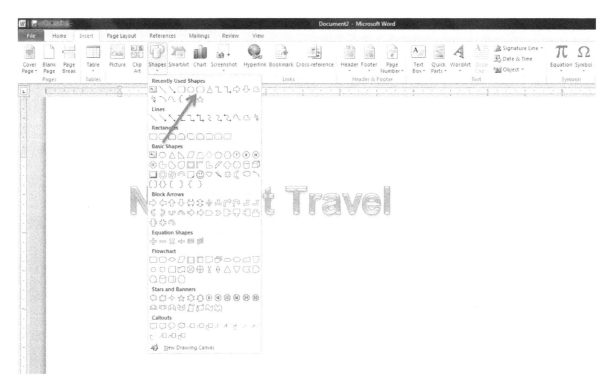

3. Click the Shapes tool in the Insert tab and choose Rounded Rectangle in the Basic Shapes section.

Now that you've selected this shape, the next step is to draw it so that is covers the WordArt text. After you have selected a shape you will then position the mouse pointer where you want the shape to begin. After locating the beginning point you will then click and drag to draw the shape.

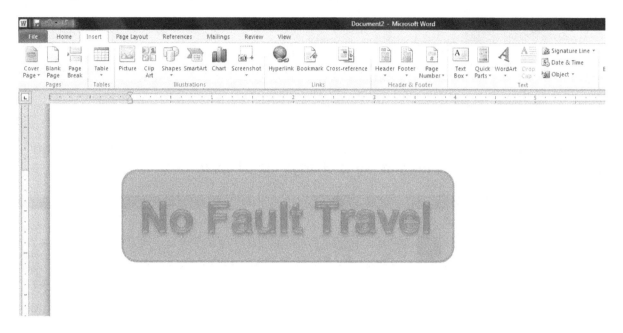

You will see the WordArt text as you drag the mouse to create the rounded rectangle.

4. Move the mouse pointer to the left and above the WordArt, then click and drag to draw a shape as shown.

When you release the mouse the rounded rectangle shape will hide the WordArt. You will correct this later. Be sure to leave plenty of rectangle to the left and right of the WordArt text. If you do not make the rounded rectangle large enough, the text will not all fit as you perform the next few steps.

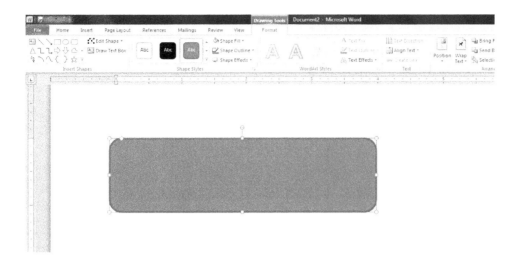

Changing Fill Color

When you draw an AutoShape, by default Word fills it with a solid color. You can use the Shape Fill tool on the Format tab to change the fill color.

1.   **Ensuring the rectangle is still selected, click the Shape Fill tool in the Shape Styles group on the ribbon. Then, select Blue, Accent 1 Lighter 80%.**

The rounded rectangle will now be light blue. You will not yet be able to see the WordArt text.

Working with 3-D Shapes

Using the Format tab on the ribbon you can add shadows and 3-D effects to the shapes you have created. In this portion of the lesson you will add a shadow effect to the rounded rectangle you have created.

1.   Ensure the rounded rectangle shape is still selected and then click the Shape Effects tool in the Shape Styles section of the ribbon.

You should now see a list of different kinds of Shape Effects you can apply to this rounded rectangle.

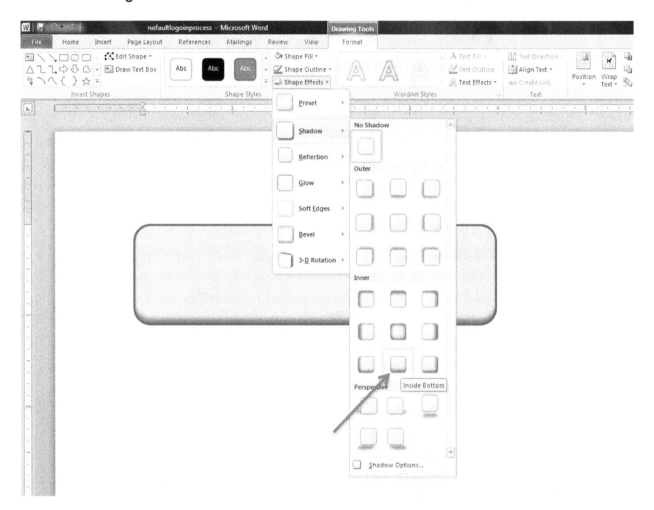

2.   Choose the Shadow option and then select Inside Bottom as the shadow style.

The image will now display the shadow effect you selected.

Changing a Shape's Layer

Word places drawing objects and shapes in layers. The first item you create will be in the first layer. Word placed the second image you inserted, the rounded rectangle, over the first object, the WordArt text. In order to see the WordArt text you must reverse the layers of these objects. You can do this by right+clicking on the object and choosing Send to Back from the shortcut menu.

1.   Right+Click the rounded rectangle.

You should now see a shortcut menu displaying commands you can use for this shape.

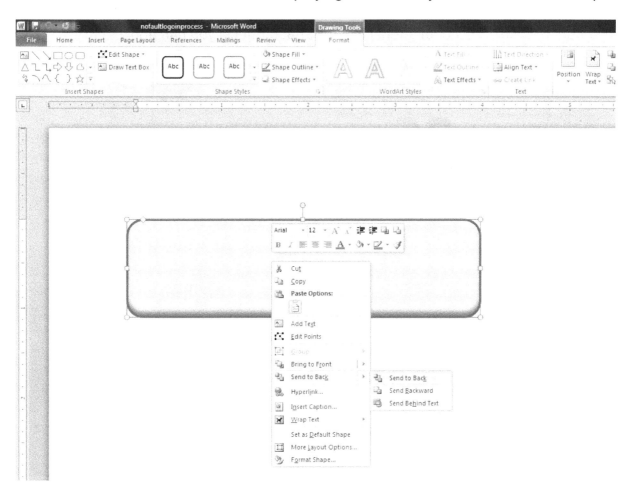

2.   From the shortcut menu click Send to Back.

You should now be able to see the WordArt within the rounded rectangle.

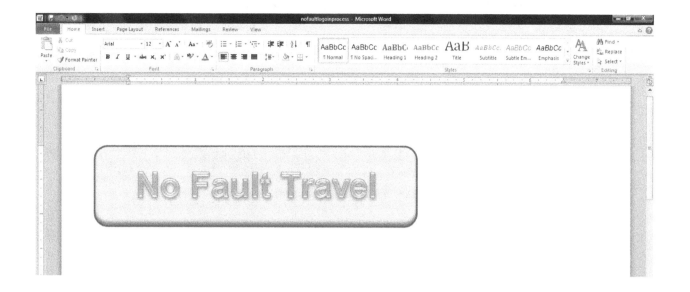

3.　Click outside the objects to de-select them.

Grouping Objects

The two shapes you created are now treated as just that, two shapes. If you wanted to copy the two shapes together, or perhaps move or size these two objects, it would be much better if Word treated the two as only one object. You can do this very easily by grouping the two objects together. To group objects, you select the objects you want to group and then right+click the selected objects. From the shortcut menu, choose Grouping.

Once grouped, you can even use the sizing handles to size both objects at the same time. You will now group the two images and eventually by using MS Paint, you will turn these two shapes into an image file.

1.　Carefully click in WordArt text.
You should now see sizing handles on just that portion of the object. Even though the back text portion does not appear to be selected, it is because it is part of the WordArt shape. If you don't succeed selecting the text the first time, click outside the objects and try again.

2.　Leaving the WordArt object selected, press and hold the (Shift) key.
You can select multiple objects by clicking with the (Shift) key depressed.

3.　With the (Shift) key depressed, click the left edge of the 3-D rectangle.
You should notice that both objects have sizing handles which tells you that both are selected.

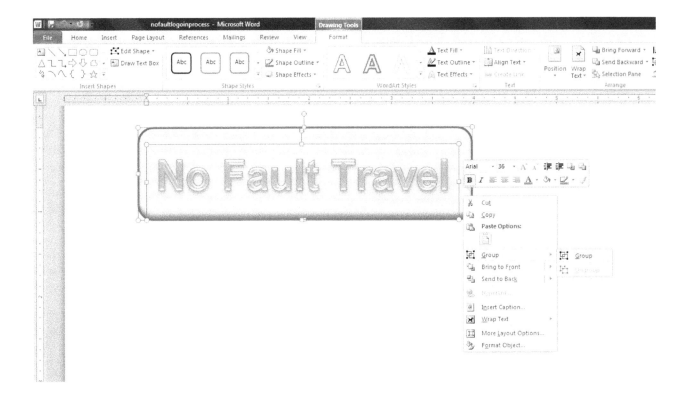

4. **Carefully right+click the selected objects. From the Shortcut menu choose Grouping and then Group.**

The objects are now grouped and Word will treat them as if they are only one object. Should you ever need to revert to two separate objects, you can ungroup grouped objects from the same shortcut menu.

Turning Objects into an Image File

If you wanted to use this image again, you could save the document that contains the image. Then, each time you wanted this image you could open the document with the image and then copy it into the document you needed it. However, it would be easier overall to save the image as an image file. Then you could insert this image as any other. In this portion of the exercise you will use MS Paint to turn the shapes into a graphic file.

1. **Make sure the grouped object is selected and then choose the Copy command.**

You know the image is selected because you see the sizing handles (white circles and squares) around it. You are now copying the image into the Windows clipboard so you can then paste it into MS Paint.

2. **Minimize Word.**

You can minimize Word either by clicking on the minimize button at the top of the window or, depending on your version of Windows, by clicking on the Word icon on the taskbar at the bottom of the screen.

3.   Start MS Paint.

If you don't have a Paint icon you can use the Start menu. From Start, go to Programs and then Accessories. Paint should be in the Accessories menu.

4.   After starting MS Paint, open the Edit menu and choose Paste.

You should now see a copy of the image in Paint. You will now save the image as a graphic file.

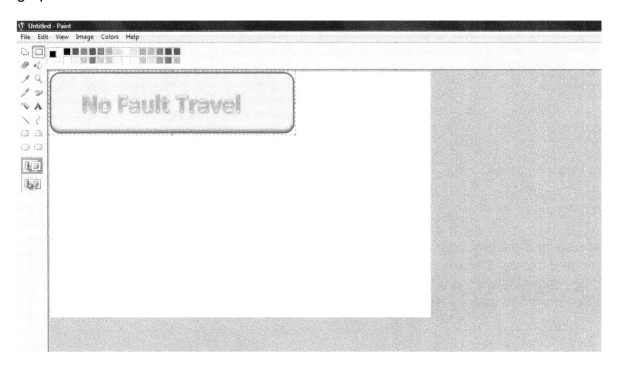

5. **Without clicking anywhere else, open the Edit menu again and choose Copy to.**

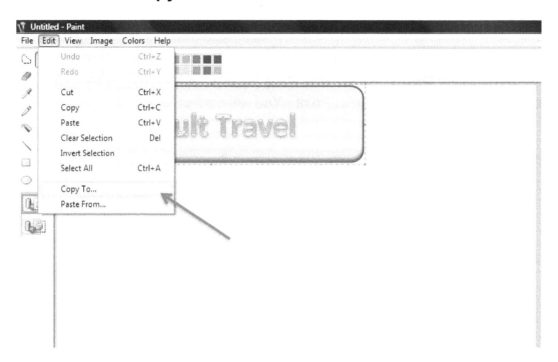

You are using the Copy To command rather than the save because you want to save only the selected image. Choosing Save would cause Paint to save the entire window, including the blank white area. This would make the image difficult to work with. The Copy To command saves just the image.

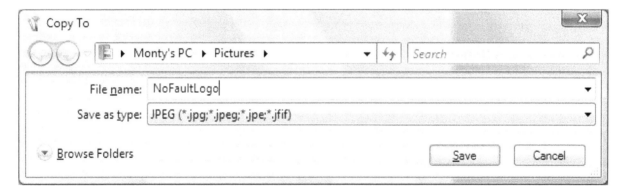

6. **In the Copy To dialog box, change folders if you want, or just leave this file in the pictures folder.**

7. **After selecting the correct folder, type *NoFault Logo* in the File name text box and click Save.**

8. **Close Paint. Choose Don't Save when asked if you want to save the file.**

You have already saved the image and do not need to save the entire file.

9. **Click the Word icon on the taskbar to restore Word.**

10. **Close the current Word document without saving.**

Once again, you have saved the image separately and do not need to save the document.

11. **Open the Travel Tales Newsletter.**

You will now replace the original logo with the new logo you just created and saved as an image file.

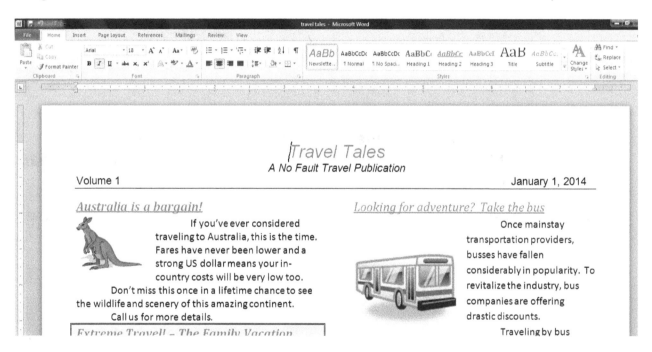

12. **Move to the top of the document and delete the existing text** *Travel Tales* **then press (Enter) two times.**

You are deleting this text because you will replace it with the graphic logo you just created.

13. **Open the Insert menu and choose Picture. Navigate to and insert the *NoFaultLogo* file you created earlier.**

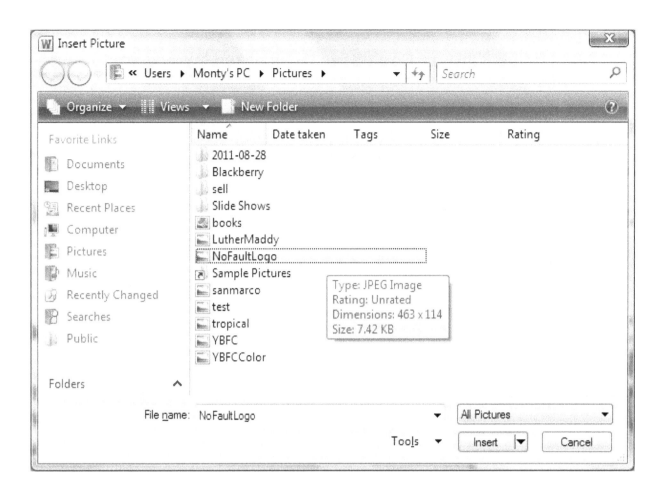

14. **Change the wrapping style to square then size and move the image to fit at the top of the page. Add the text to make is appear as shown.**

15. **Save and then close the newsletter file.**

Working with Diagrams

Word allows you to easily create several pre-formatted diagrams. You can insert diagrams by displaying the Insert tab and choosing Diagram. Then, in the Diagram gallery, you can choose the diagram you want to insert. In this portion of the lesson you will create an organizational chart for No Fault Travel.

1. In a new, blank document, display the Insert tab, click the Smart Art Tool and choose Hierarchy.

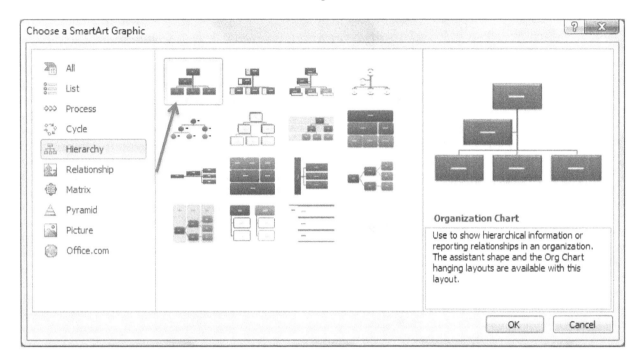

2. In the choices of Hierarchy diagrams, choose Organizational Chart and OK.

Word will now insert an organizational chart into the document. . You can now add text to the shapes, change shape colors or insert additional shapes.

3. Add text to the shapes so the diagram appears as that on the next page.

You can do this easily by typing in the *Text pane.* Click the mouse to select each shape in the "Type your text here" section. You can use the mouse to move from one shape to the next.

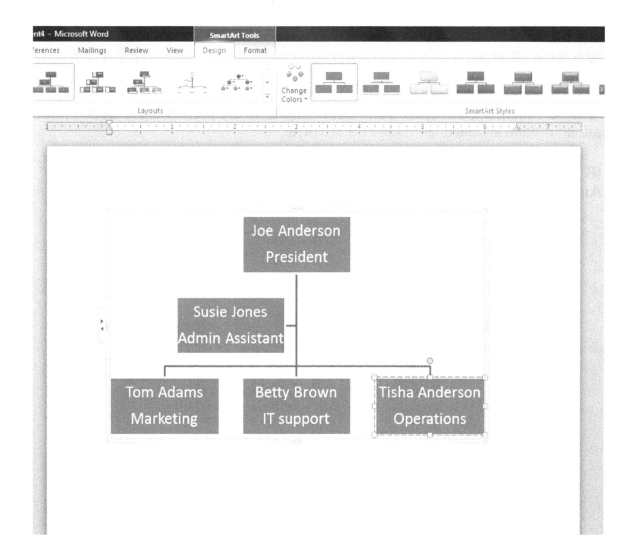

Adding shapes

Now, we'll add some additional employees to this org chart.

4.   **In the Organization chart, right+click on Joe Anderson's shape to select it. Then choose Add Shape and then choose Add Shape Below.**

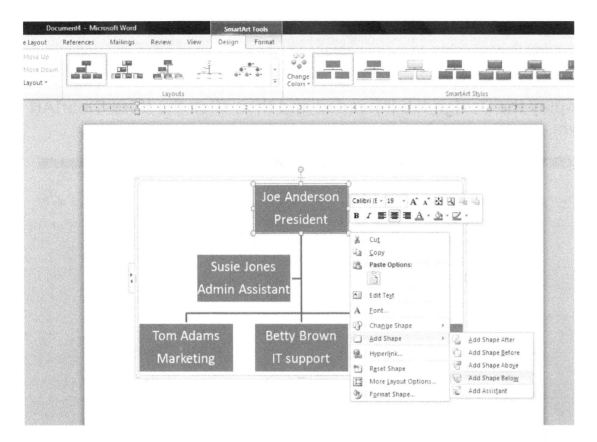

You have now added another shape to the diagram. This shape reports to the president in the hierarchy.

5.   Add text to the new shape that reads, *Mark Anderson Engineering.*

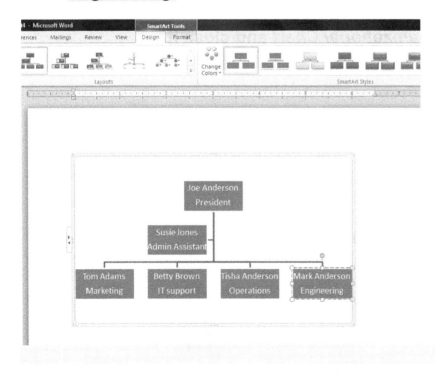

Changing Styles

Word allows you to easily change the appearance of the diagram you just inserted by selecting a style.

6.   Display the Design tab if needed and then click the third SmartArt style.

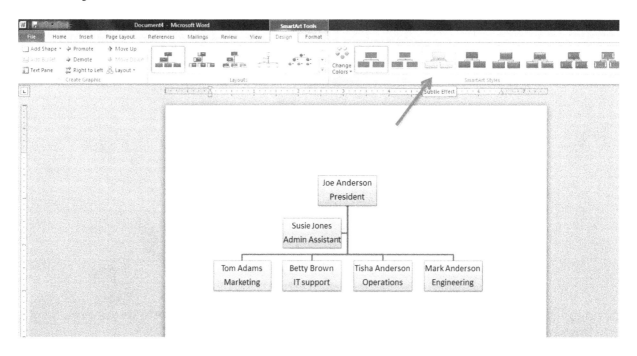

The Organizational chart should now be formatted in this style.

7.   Save this file as *Organizational Chart* and close it.

1. Open Joes's Newsletter.

2. Use WordArt and Basic shapes to create the logo as shown.

Hint: Don't forget to group the objects so you can size and move them as one.

Also, to make the WordArt appear similar to the that below, try experimenting with the Text Effects, Transform tool on the WordArt styles tab.

Classes for the Masses

Volume 8   June 1, 1999

Intro to computers will get you going

 Don't know a mouse from a rat? If not, sign up for our Intro to computers class. We'll have you counting bits and bytes in no time. Call for details.

New Versions released daily!

It seems just when you get a software package learned, the company releases a new and entirely different version. If you find yourself struggling to learn a new version of a program you used to know, give us a call. We'll get you back to the comfortable stage.

Voice input making progress

 More and more companies are releasing voice input devices and software. Their ultimate goal is to someday replace the keyboard. While the current devices are good if you have no keyboard skills at all, they still have a way to go to replace the keyboard entirely. In the meantime, keep practicing your typing.

3. Save and close when done.

Lesson #4: Enhancing Labels

In this lesson you will learn to:

Add graphic images to labels
Capture screens
Crop images

Lesson #4: Enhancing Labels

If you are sending documents in the mail, you probably want them to be opened and read. One way to do this is to help your mailing documents stand out from the rest of the large pile of mail your customers or others may receive daily. In this portion of the lesson you'll create return address labels for No Fault Travel. These labels will contain a graphic image to dress up the mail you send out.

1.   Open Word and display a new, empty document.

2.   From the Mailings tab, click the Labels tool.

You will now see the Envelopes and Labels dialog box. Here you will tell Word what brand and size of label you are using.

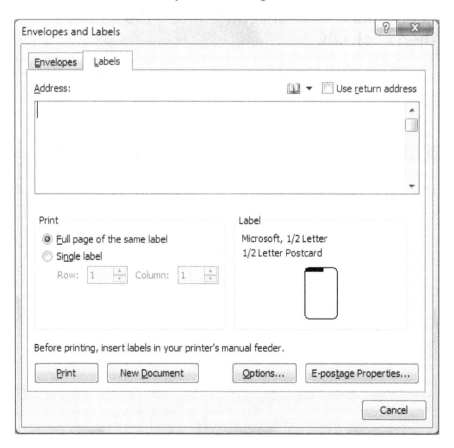

3.   Ensure the Labels tab is selected, then click the options button.

You will now need to select the manufacturer of the label you are using and the size or model number. For this lesson, we'll assume you are using Avery 5160, which is the standard size mailing label.

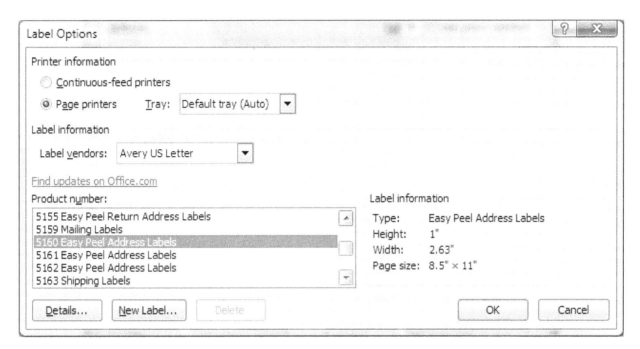

4.   Choose Avery US Letter as the label vendor and 5160 as the product number, then click OK.

You will now return to the Envelopes and Labels dialog box. Here you should notice that Avery 5160 is shown as the label choice. You will now tell Word that you want to edit an entire sheet of labels.

5.   In the Envelopes and Labels dialog box, click New Document.

You should now see an entire sheet of blank labels. If you do not see the outline of the labels, display the Layout tab of the Table tools section of the Ribbon and click the View Gridlines tool.

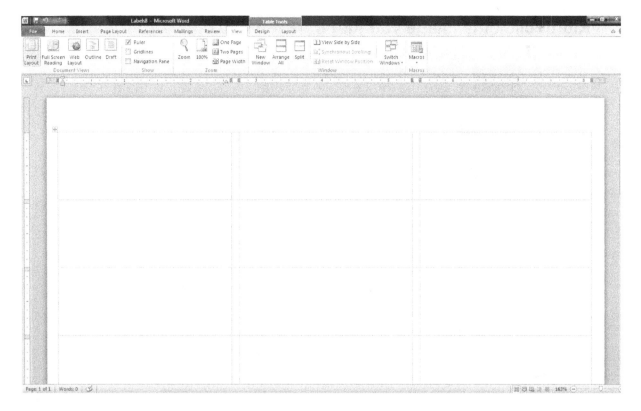

The next step is to create one label as we want it to appear. Then we'll copy that label into the remaining labels on the page to create an entire sheet of enhanced labels. We'll start enhancing this label by adding a clipart image.

6.   Display the Insert tab and click the ClipArt tool.

7.   Type *travel* in the search for textbox in the clipart pane and insert the image, or similar, as shown.

Now you'll resize this image so there is room to type the return address on this label.

8. Right+click the image you just inserted and choose Size and Position from the shortcut menu.

The method you choose to size the image does not matter. This is just the procedure we're taking here.

8. Ensuring the Lock aspect ratio option is on, change the height to .5" and click OK.

The image you just inserted should now appear with the size you just selected. Now, to be able to have text appear beside the label, you'll need to change its wrapping style.

9. With the image selected, click the Wrap Text tool in the Format tab and choose Square.

Now, you'll add the address to the first label and then copy it to the other labels in the sheet.

10. In the first label enter the name and address as shown:

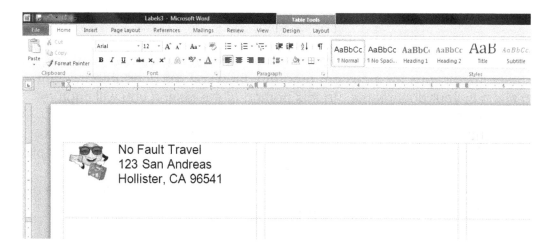

The next step is to select this cell and then copy its contents into the other labels.

11. Select the contents of the first cell by clicking and dragging and then choose the Copy command.

Make sure you select the image as well. You can also easily select the cell by moving out of it and then back into the cell with Shift+Tab.

12. Move to each empty label and paste.

Remember the shortcut key for paste is Control+V. Using this makes the process a little faster.

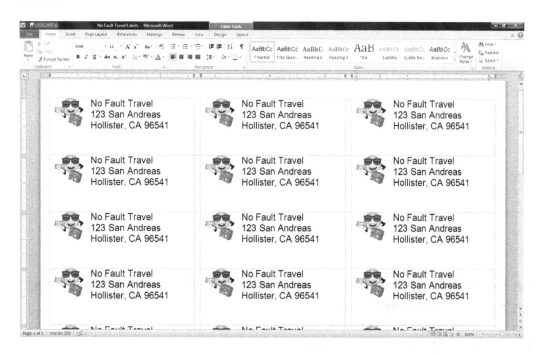

13. **Save this document as *No Fault Travel Labels* and close it.**

The next time you need these labels just open the document and print. At home, this process is great for making labels for Christmas cards or any other return address label you want to enhance.

Capturing Screens

If you are ever tasked with creating documentation for anything computer based, say for example, user instructions for a custom program, then you will undoubtedly want to include screen shots in your documents. In this portion of the lesson you will capture entire screens and active dialog boxes.

To capture an entire screen you simply press the (Print Screen) key. This places an image of the entire screen into the Windows clipboard. To use the screen shot, simply choose Paste to paste the screen into the desired document.

To capture just the active dialog box, you press (Alt + Print Screen). This places an image of that dialog box in the Windows clipboard. The Paste command will place the image in the current document.

For example purposes this lesson will assume you need to create simple instructions on changing fonts in Word. You will use some screen shots to create this document.

Word 2010 has added a screen capture option, Screenshot, on the Insert tab and in this lesson you will use both this feature and the (Alt+Print Screen) to capture just a portion of the screen. You will assume you are creating user instructions for changing fonts in Microsoft Word 2010.

1. **In a new document type the following: *Click the Font dialog box launcher* and then press (Enter) twice.**

You would now like to include a screen shot that shows the open Format Menu.

2. **Click the Font dialog box launcher to display the Font dialog box and then press (Alt+Print Screen).**

You are capturing just this dialog box, not the entire screen.
You have now placed an image of this dialog box in the clipboard.

3.   Click below the text you typed in this document and then click the drop down list button for the Paste tool.

You should now see an image of the screen pasted into the document

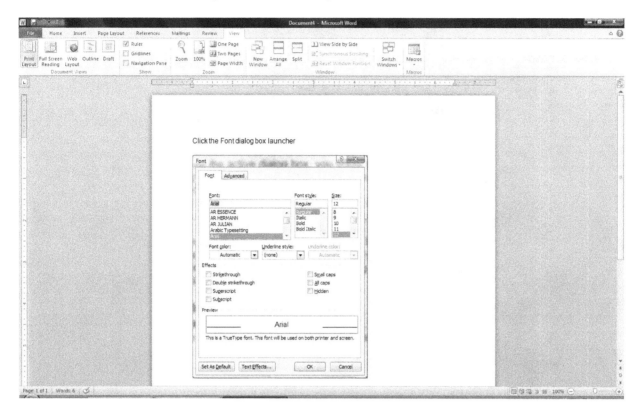

Now you'll use the Screenshot tool to capture an entire screen and add it to the second page of the document.

4.   Create a new document with (Control+N).
If you created a new document using another method, it will not matter.

5.   Navigate back to the document with the font dialog box screen shot, leaving the new document open.
How you do this will depend on your version of Windows, but you can use the windows Taskbar to do this.

6.   Move to the bottom of the document and create a new page with (Control+Enter).

7.   At the top of this page type: *The Word 2010 window* and press Enter.

Now you're ready to insert a screen shot of the blank document you just created. You won't have to press the Print Screen key because Word 2010 automatically captures screens for you.

8.   Display the Insert Tab and click the Screenshot tool. Click on the image of the new blank document you just created.

You should now see an image of that window in your document.

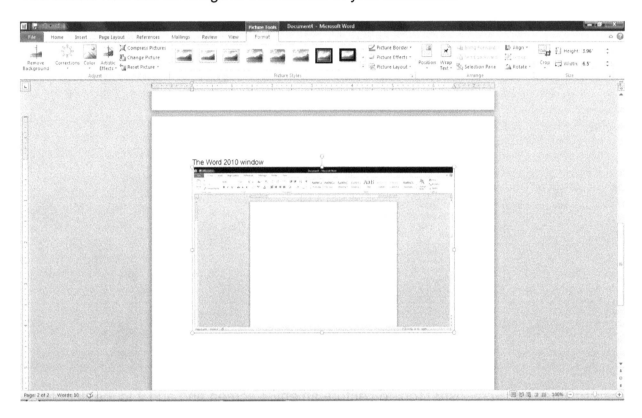

Now, you'll create another page and learn to use the Crop feature to remove portions of a screenshot you may not want.

9.   Create a third page to this document and type: *The Word 2010 Ribbon* and press (Enter).

Now, you'll insert the same blank document Word window and then crop away everything but the Ribbon.

10.   Use the Screenshot tool to insert the blank Word document image on this page.

11.   Display the Format tab and click the Crop tool.

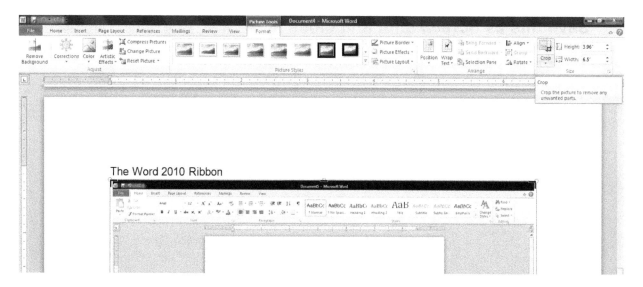

After clicking the Crop tool, you should notice that Word has added some black bars at the location of each sizing handle. You will use these as cropping handles to tell Word how much of the image you want to crop away.

12.   Locate the bottom center cropping handle and drag up until only the Ribbon is not grayed out as shown below.

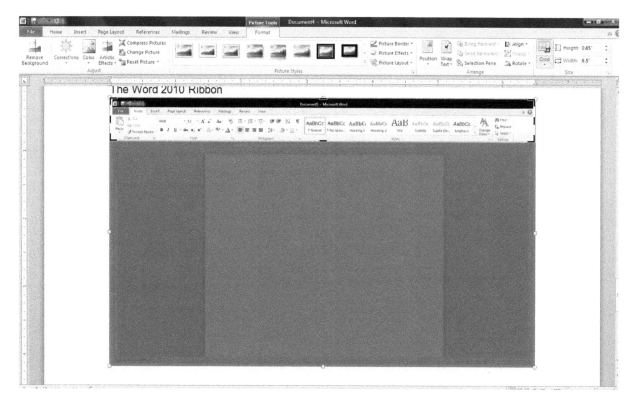

13.   Click the Crop tool again to complete the crop.

After clicking the Crop tool again, the image now resets to display only the portion you did not crop.

14. Save this as *Screen shot* and close it.

1.   Open Joe's Newsletter.

2.   Add a screen shot of the desktop to the bottom of the newsletter as shown below.

Your desktop will look different from that below. Also, you will likely need to use the PrintScreen key to insert this image rather than Word's Screenshot tool.

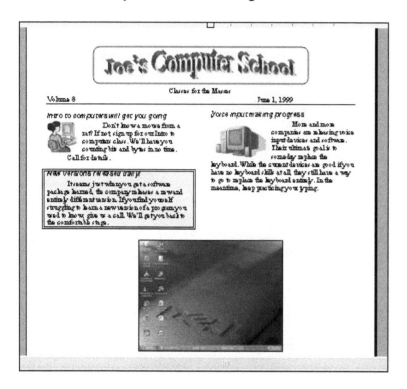

3.   Save and close all open documents when done.

Lesson #5: Page Enhancements

In this lesson you will learn to:

Add Page Borders
Add Custom Watermarks
Add Page colors

Lesson #5: Page Enhancements

Up to this point you have learned how to change the appearance of paragraphs and other portions of text. In this lesson you'll learn to use features that enhance the entire page.

1. Start with a blank document.

2. Insert a clipart image similar to that shown below.

You may use the search term Hawaii to find this or similar image in your clipart gallery.

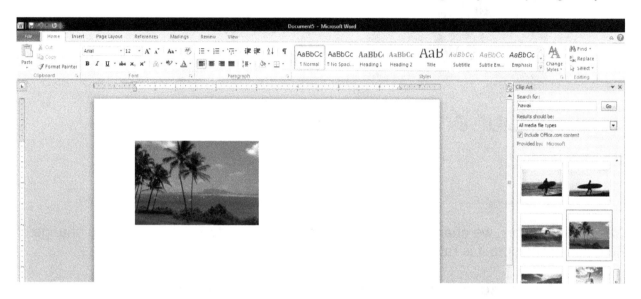

3. Resize the image to be exactly 2" tall and change the text wrapping style to square.

Remember you can right+click the image and choose Size and Position to access both of these image options.

4. Move to the end of the document with Control+End and press (Enter) once.

If you do not move to the end of the document before pressing (Enter) it is likely the image you just inserted will move down the page. Moving here prevents that from happening.

5. Change the font to Arial 28 points, center and type, *No Fault Travel* and then press (Enter).

6.   Continue creating the document as shown below.

When creating this, we changed the "annual sale" line to a dark red font. If you change the color, make sure it is rather dark or it will disappear in the next few steps.

6.   Add one more line below that reads, *Call for details today.*

To keep this lesson simple, we won't have you complete an entire flyer, just enough to show you how to learn the features in this chapter. When you're creating your own flyers, you can then enhance them as you like.

Adding a Page Border

In an earlier lesson you learned how to add borders to a paragraph. Now, you're going to add a border for the entire page. And, to make it even more impressive, you'll use the Art border feature.

1.   Display the Page Layout tab and click the Page Borders tool.

You should now see the Borders and Shading dialog box. Here you can select from several different line styles and even change line's thickness and color. However, this time, you'll add a graphic border.

1. **In the Borders and Shading dialog box, click the Art drop down list in the Page Border section. Then scroll down to and select the colorful palm trees. Click OK when done.**

When you return to the document you should see the art border around the entire page.

Page Colors

Now that you've added a page border, the next step in enhancing this document will be to change the color of the entire page. You can do this very easily with the Page Color tool just to the left of the Page Borders tool.

1.   Click the Page Color tool in the Page Background group.

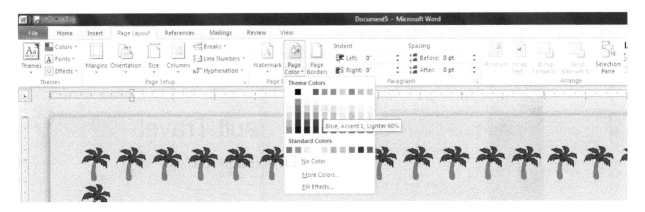

2.   Select Blue, Accent 1 as the page color.

We are selecting a light color so our current text will still be visible on the page.

Adding Watermarks

Watermarks are very lightly printed messages on the page. They may be used to specify that a document is confidential, or is simply a draft copy. Word allows you to create custom watermarks with your own text, or even use an image as a watermark. You'll have to experiment with these on your own. For now, we'll just have you add a watermark to this document specifying that it is a Draft copy. You add watermarks using the Watermark tool in the Page Background group.

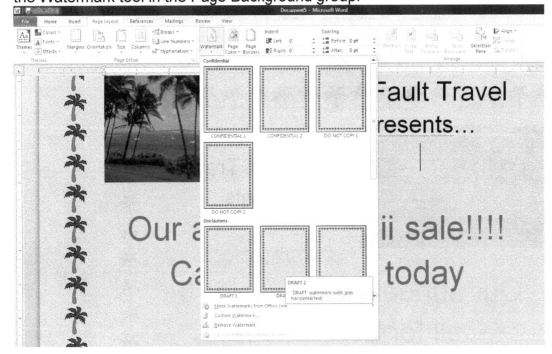

Had you not already added a page color, you would see the words in the watermark thumbnails. Word will automatically adjust the font color of the watermark so it will show on the page.

1.   Click the Watermark tool and choose the Draft 2 watermark.

Word has now added a "Draft" watermark to this document. To create your own custom watermark, you can select Custom Watermark instead of choosing one of the pre-defined watermarks as you just did.

Ensuring the Page Color will Print

With some installations of Word 2010, the command that allows the page color to print is turned off. We'll now have you go through the steps to turn this feature on, or at least ensure that it is already turned on before you print this document.

1.   Click File to display the File menu, then choose Options.

Word will now display the Word Options dialog box. Here you will choose the Display options and ensure the page colors print.

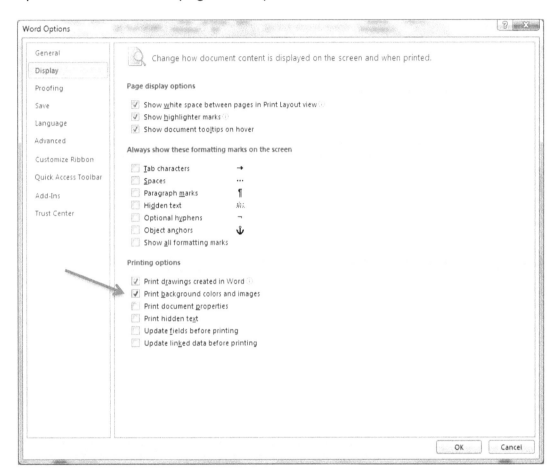

2.   In the Word Options dialog box, click Display.

3.   If not already on, turn on the *Print background color and images* check box and click OK.

Now, when you print this document, the color background will print.

4.   Save this document as *Hawaii Sale* and then close it.

Using Pre-defined Templates

Learning to create flyers and other advertising documents on your own allows you to have an end product that looks exactly how you want it. However, there are sometimes when it is helpful to let someone else do all the work, especially when you don't have a lot of time to spend creating your own documents. Such is the case with Word templates. There are numerous pre-defined templates for just about everything from professional marketing flyers to advertising a yard sale. In this portion of this lesson you'll download and then customize a predefined Word template.

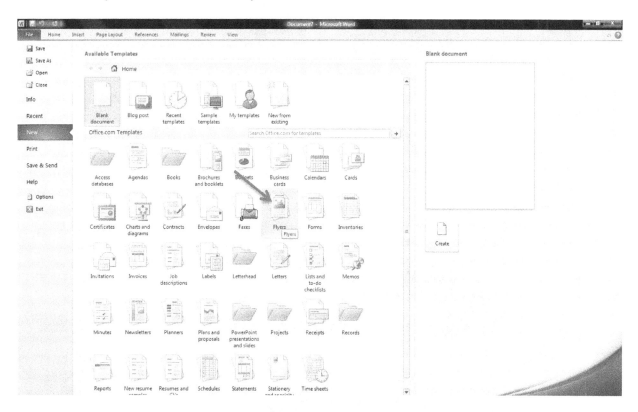

1. **From a new document, open the File menu and choose New. Then, in the list of templates, select Flyers.**

Word will now display several categories of flyer templates.

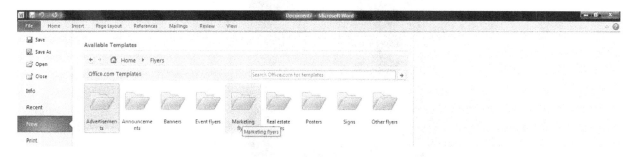

2. **Choose Marketing flyers.**

Word will now open the Marketing Flyers folder and display all the available marketing flyer templates. You will now select the flyer you want to use.

3.   Scroll down to and select the Sale event flyer and then click download.

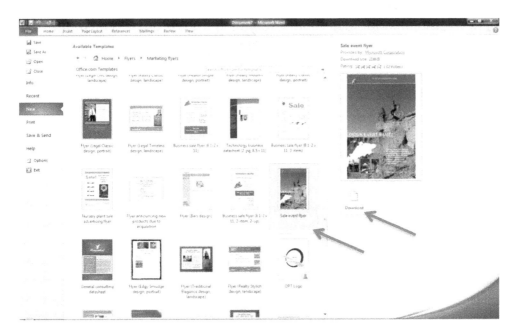

As soon as you click download, Word will create a new document based on this template. The next step is to customize the text to make it personal.

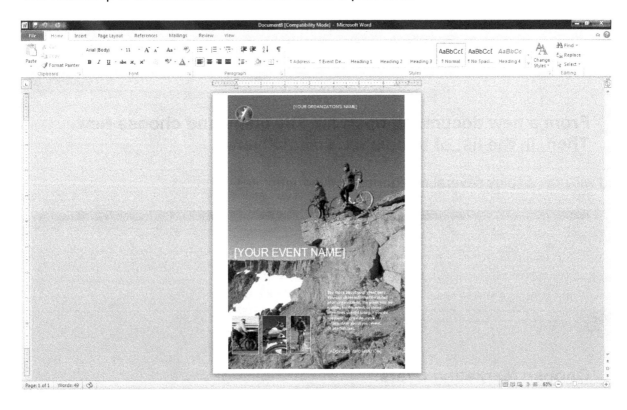

4. **Select the text in the "Your Organization's Name" text box and replace it with, *No Fault Travel*.**

After typing this text you can experiment with different font sizes. The example image in this book used Arial 26 point type.

The next step is to enter your custom text in the Event Name section.

5. **Select the text in the "Event name" text box and replace it with, *Bike Southern Utah!***

You can quickly select the text you want to replace by triple clicking in it. You'll also replace the "Say more about your event" section with custom text.

6. **Change the "Say more about your event" to read:**
   Whether it's Zion, Bryce or Moab, you can't beat Sothern Utah for bicycling.
   Call today to reserve the trip of a lifetime!

7. **In the "Address Information" section type: *800-555-5656*.**

Hopefully you now have an idea of some of the impressive templates available for you to use in Word. Don't give up making some documents on your own, but there is an impressive list of templates here. Learning some of the features covered in this book should help you when you need to change some of the features on pre-defined templates.

8. **Save this flyer as *Southern Utah Bike Flyer* and close it.**

A note on printing: You probably noticed the backgrounds for both the bike flyer and the Hawaii sale did not stretch across the entire screen. This happens because most printers cannot print to the edges and must reserve some area on each edge for a non-printable margin. If you wanted to use this document in a situation where you needed it to print edge to edge, you may be able to save the document as a PDF file (Save As) and then take the file to a printer or office super store. Often their printers will print to the edges (full bleed) and this way you can still use Word to create your documents but just have some of them professionally printed.

1.   Create a document using a blank template that appears at that shown.

This template is in the Marketing Flyers folder.

3.   Save and close all open documents when done.

Lesson #5: Working with Hyperlinks

In this lesson you will learn to:

Create and modify hyperlinks
Use the Paste as Hyperlink command

Lesson #5: Working with Hyperlinks

A hyperlink allows you to go from one place to another quickly by simply clicking on "linked text". Hyperlinks can be internal, which take you to another place within the same document, or external, which take you to some place outside the document you are currently in. External hyperlinks may take you to a place on the Internet, or may simply open another MS Office document.

Creating Hyperlinks is very easy. First, you type the text you want displayed as the link. Then, you select the text and choose Insert Hyperlink. Word will then allow you to specify the location

Automatically Creating External Hyperlinks

Unless you have turned this feature off, Word will automatically create a hyperlink when you type something it recognizes as a web site address or email address. After you type this text, you will notice that Word changes the font color to blue and underlines the text. This is the standard formatting for hyperlinks.

1. **Open the Travel Tales Newsletter.**

2. **Go to the bottom of the document with (Control+end). Press (Enter) until you are below the logo. Then, type *For more information, visit our web site at: www.NoFaultTravel.com* and press (Enter).**

You should notice the color change and underlining for the web address. Word has now created a hyperlink to that web address. If you click the hyperlink, Word will start your internet browser and try to locate that web site. However, since this site does not exist, you will receive an error message. If you had typed an actual web address, you could now quickly get to that site from this newsletter document.

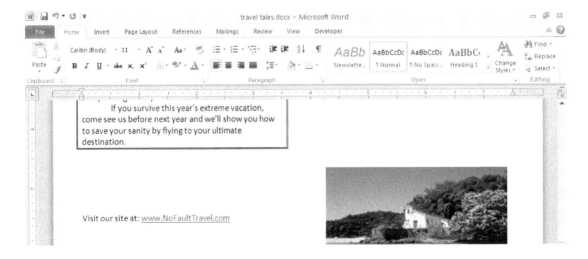

Editing or Removing Hyperlinks

After you've created a hyperlink, either manually or automatically, you can easily edit or even remove the hyperlink attached to the text. One way to accomplish this is to carefully right+click on the hyperlink text and then choose either Edit or Delete from the shortcut menu.

1.   Move the mouse pointer into the hyperlink text and right+click.

Word will now display a shortcut menu.

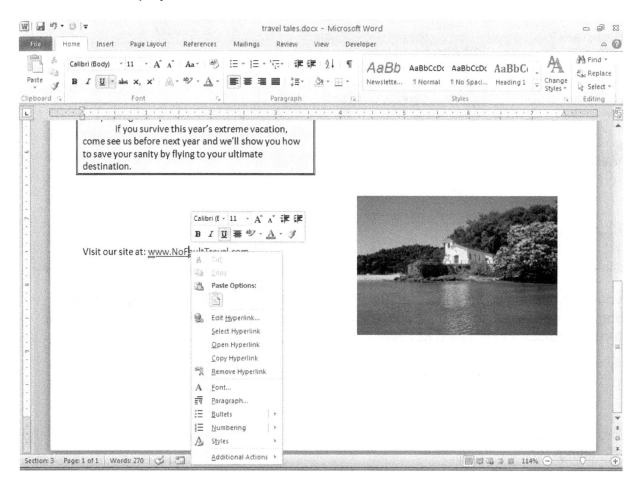

2.   Choose Edit Hyperlink from the Shortcut menu.

You should now see the Edit Hyperlink dialog box. Here you can change the address that a Hyperlink goes to when you click it.

3. **Change the text in the Address text box from www.NoFaultTravel.com to www.Expedia.com. Next, change the Text to display to No Fault Travel and click OK.**

Note: We are not endorsing Expedia, just simply using it for example purposes as a "real" website we can go to when trying out a hyperlink.

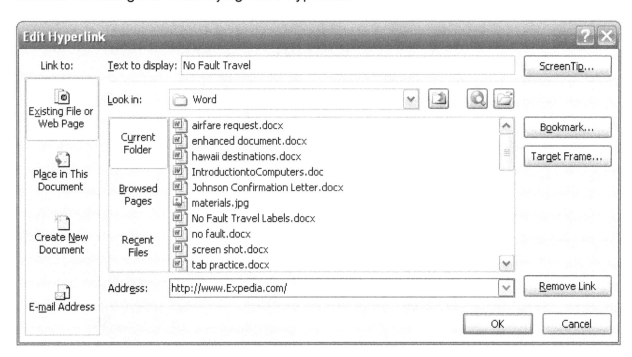

If your computer is attached to the Internet, try out the hyperlink by holding down the Control key and clicking on the hyperlink text. If you have an Internet connection, your Internet browser should go to that site.

4. **Right+click the hyperlinked text and choose Remove Hyperlink from the shortcut menu.**

Word has now removed the hyperlink from the text. It also removed the color change and underlining.

5. **Save the *Travel Tales* newsletter.**

Using the Paste As Link

In this portion of the exercise you will add a hyperlink that links to a file on your computer rather than an internet site. To create a link in one document to another document you must include the entire path and filename, *C:\my documents\word files\Travel Tales*, for example, may be the path to this document. Creating hyperlinks this way can lead to errors resulting from forgetting the correct path or from typos. An easier way to create hyperlinks to a file is to use the Paste as Link feature. When you use this feature, Word inserts the correct path into the hyperlink automatically.

1.   **In the Travel Tales newsletter, move to and select the date of the newsletter, *January 1, 2014.***
This will be the text that the hyperlink you are about to create will display.

2.   **With this text selected, choose the Copy command and then create a new document with (Control+N).**

3.   **In the new blank document, center and type *Newsletter Directory* press (enter) twice then change the justification back to Left.**

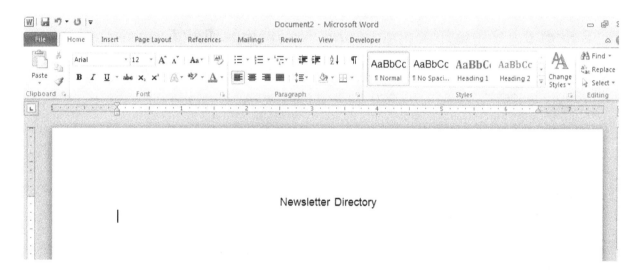

4.   **Click the Paste tool drop down list and choose Paste Special.**

You should see the Paste Special dialog box. Here you can tell Word that you want to paste the text you just copied and have it link back to the original document.

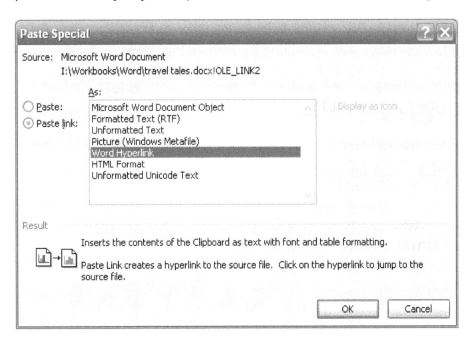

5. **Select the Paste link option and Word Hyperlink format, then click OK.**

You should now have returned to the newsletter directory document. You should also see that Word inserted the text you copied as a hyperlink.

6. **Close the Travel Tales newsletter but keep the "directory" document you just pasted the text into open.**

You will now try out the hyperlink you just created it. If it works correctly, Word should open the Travel Tales document when you follow the hyperlink in this directory.

7. **Press and hold (Control) then click the hyperlink. Choose Yes if Word security options ask if you would like to proceed.**

Word should now open the closed Newsletter file.

8. **Close the Travel Tales newsletter.**

9. **Save this document as *Newsletter directory* and then close it.**

© Luther M. Maddy III

www.ingramcontent.com/pod-product-compliance
Lightning Source LLC
Chambersburg PA
CBHW060455060326
40689CB00020B/4544